Has your family got a car?

Cars are very common indeed. In fact, there are more cars on the planet than there are houses. That is a lot of cars!

Not all of the cars are in use.

old, rusty cars in a junkyard

Some of the old and unused cars are just left to rust, but some are broken down. The metal can then be used to make more modern cars.

cars waiting to be taken apart

These are the main parts of a car.

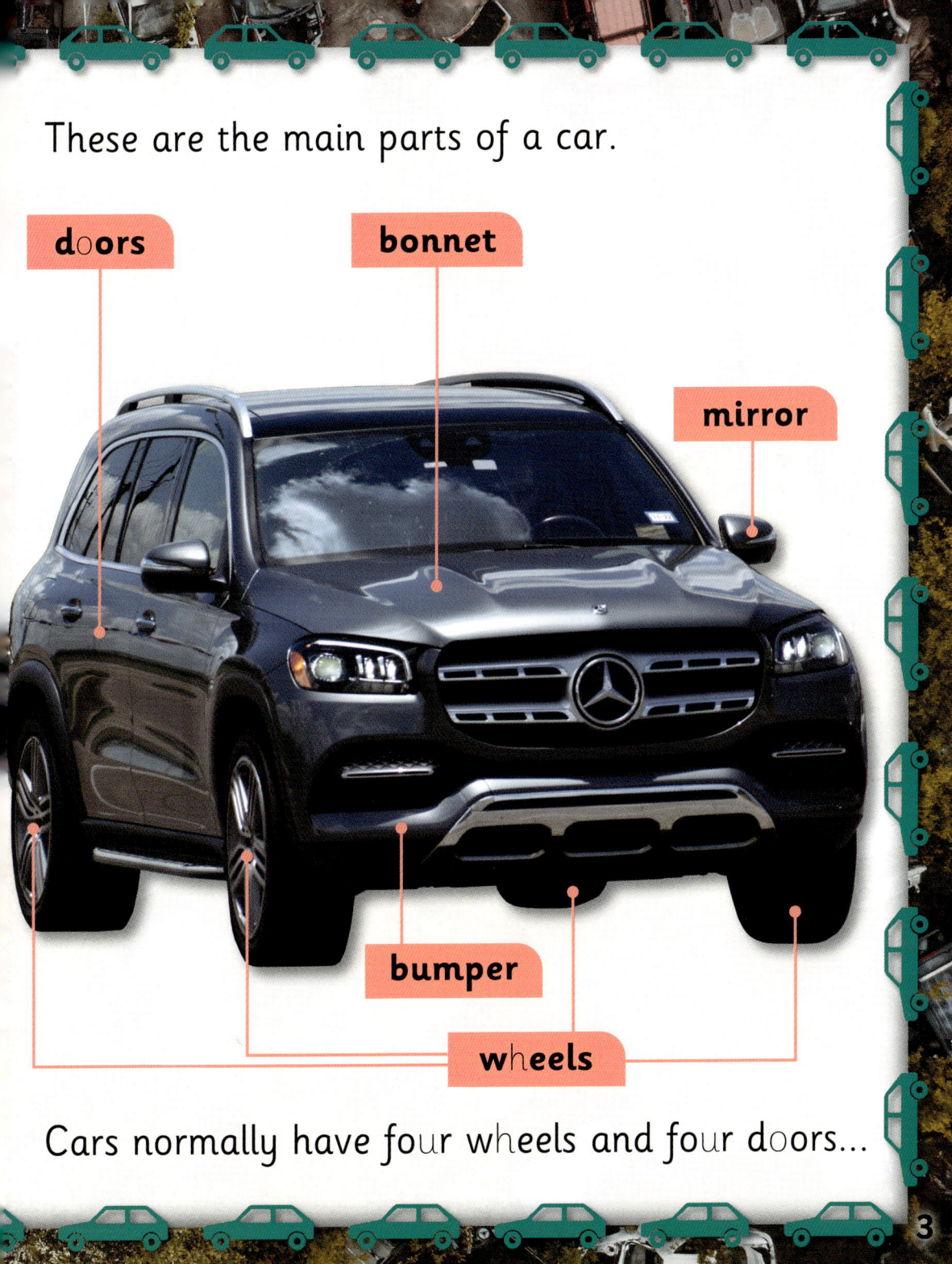

doors

bonnet

mirror

bumper

wheels

Cars normally have four wheels and four doors...

But they do not have to. In fact, cars can come in lots of different shapes and sizes.

This car only has room for the driver and one more person. It is a bit of a squeeze!

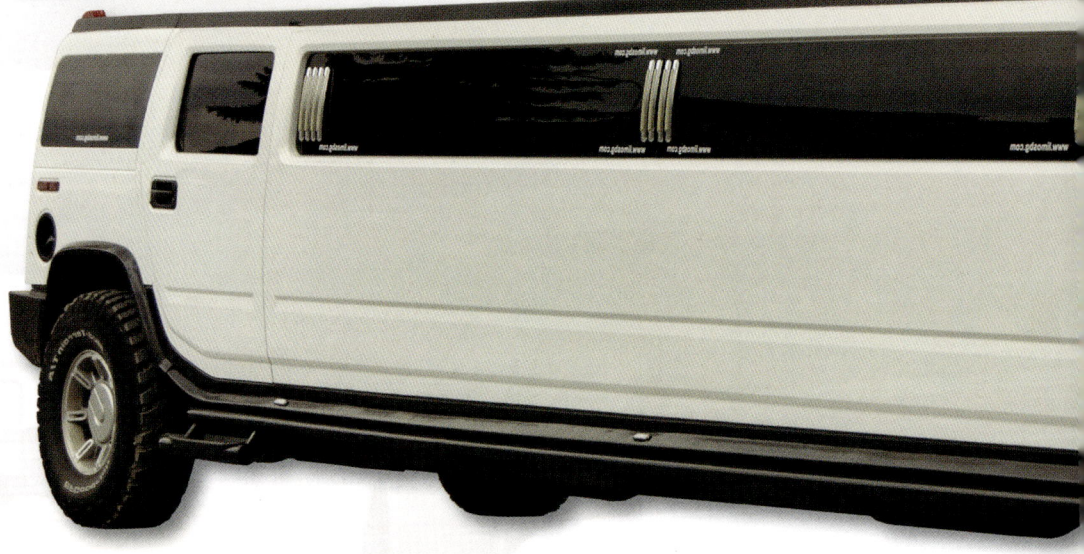

While this car is enormous, with lots of room inside.

This is an F1 racing (/**rai**sing/) car. It is built for speed.

These cars are incredibly slick and quick.

5

You are not very likely to see extremely long or small cars on our roads. Instead, you are more likely to see common cars, such as hatchbacks, saloons, SUVs and sports cars.

A hatchback is normally quite a small car.

A saloon tends to be longer.

Sports cars are very expensive.

Some cars are convertible. They have a roof that can fold down.

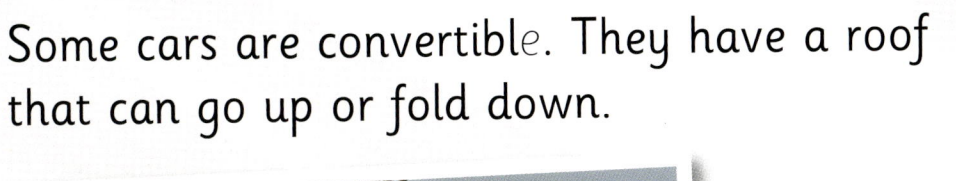

roof up

roof going down

roof down

Sometimes a convertible roof is made from hard things, like plastic or metal, and sometimes it is made from soft things, like fabric.

Not everyone likes modern cars. Some drivers prefer older classic cars.

a classic car

Drivers of classic cars are often interested in art and history. They like the look of the old cars.

These classic car drivers are meeting up for a drive in the countryside called a classic car rally. This sort of rally is not about being speedy. You have to complete the rally at the same speed as everyone else.

As well as cars, we have vans, trucks, lorries and buses on our roads.

This is a camper van. It has a little cabin at the back for sleeping in.

Small vans like this can be used to deliver mail.

Pick-up trucks like this are often used for carrying heavy objects.

Big lorries like this are used to transport goods across the country.

This is a British bus called a double-decker. It has two floors.

This is an American school bus. It takes children to school.

With all of these cars, vans and buses on our roads, there are often traffic jams.

heavy traffic

A traffic jam is when there is a long line of cars on a road. Sometimes all of the cars in the traffic jam have had to stop completely.

The longest traffic jam ever was 109 (a hundred and nine) miles (or 175km) long. That is a long line of cars!

We can all avoid sitting in traffic jams by travelling on foot or on our bikes as much as possible.

When there are a lot of drivers on a road, everyone needs to know where they can go and when.

These road markings tell the drivers which side of the road to drive on.

While this marking tells drivers that only bikes can use this lane.

These are traffic signals. We have them where roads meet to tell some cars to go and some cars to stop. This helps to keep everyone safe.

Amber is for get ready to stop; red is for stop; red and amber is for get ready to go; and green is for go.

Cars are useful, but they are not perfect. All cars — even electric ones — pollute (harm) the planet. To combat this, we need to use them as little as possible.

thick car fumes

Public transport, bikes and travelling on foot are all better than going by car.